CHI

EARTH ALERT!

Rivers

Shelagh Whiting

HODDER
Wayland

an imprint of Hodder Children's Books

WWF

Produced in Association with WWF UK

Earth Alert!

Coasts
Energy
Farming

Settlements
Transport
Rivers

Cover: Pollution on a river bank.
Title page: Dead fish in an Australian river.
Contents page: Beavers build dams across streams and small rivers. Behind the dam it builds a 'lodge' of sticks and mud. Banff National Park, Canada.

First published in Great Britain in 1998 by Wayland Publishers Ltd
This paperback edition published in 2001 by Hodder Wayland,
an imprint of Hodder Children's Books
© Hodder Wayland 1998

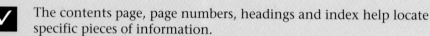

All Hodder Wayland books encourage children to read and help them improve their literacy.

✓ The contents page, page numbers, headings and index help locate specific pieces of information.

✓ The glossary reinforces alphabetic knowledge and extends vocabulary.

✓ The further information section suggests other books dealing with the same subject.

WWF UK is a registered charity no. 1081247
WWF UK, Panda House, Weyside Park, Godalming,
Surrey GU7 1XR

British Library Cataloguing in Publication Data
Whiting, Shelagh
  Rivers. – (Earth alert)
  1. Rivers – Juvenile literature 2. Stream ecology – Juvenile
  literature
  I. Title
  551.4'83

ISBN 0 7502 3377 X

Designed by: Open Book
Printed in Hong Kong

This book was prepared for
Wayland Publishers Ltd
by Margot Richardson,
23 Hanover Terrace, Brighton, E Sussex, BN2 2SN

Picture acknowledgements
Axiom Photographic Agency (Jim Holmes) 12, (Chris Coe) 25; Clearwater Projects/Allyson Bizer 27; James Davis Travel Photography 24; Ecoscene (Alexandra Jones) 1, (Anthony Cooper) 3, (Frank Blackburn) 9 bottom, (Anthony Cooper) 9 top, (Alexandra Jones) 16, (Erik Schaffer) 17, (Paul Ferraby) 20, (Jim Winkley) 22, (Nick Hawkes) 23, (John Wilkinson) 26; Eye Ubiquitous (David Cumming) 11, (L. Fordyce) 15, (David Cumming) 18, 28; Impact Photos (Robert Gibbs) 4, (Marco Siqueira) 10, (Michael George) 27; Popperfoto (Marcelo del Pozo) 19; Wayland (David Cumming) 5, (Julia Waterlow) 6, 13 top, (Julia Waterlow) 14 and 16; Shelagh Whiting 7, 13 bottom. Artwork by Peter Bull Art Studio.

The author and publishers would like to thank Allyson Bizer for her kind assistance with this book.

Contents

What is a River?

Waterfalls are found where rivers flow over steps of hard rock.

A river is a large stream of fresh water flowing in a channel. Rivers flow downhill towards the sea, a lake, a marsh or another river. They are like a 'corridor', linking hills, lowlands and coasts. They may flow through many regions, or even many countries. River environments are extremely important to the earth because all life needs water to survive.

Fresh and salt water

Ninety-seven per cent of the earth's water is salty. Only 3 per cent of water is fresh, but nearly two-thirds of that is permanently frozen in ice caps at the North and South Poles. This leaves only 1 per cent. It includes all the water in rivers and lakes, and all the drinking water in the world.

For such a large planet, the fresh water that can be used is a very tiny amount. Life can survive only because this water is constantly recycled. Every drop of water on the earth has been used over and over again since time began. This natural recycling system is called the water cycle.

The water cycle

Water is constantly evaporating from the surface of the earth, oceans, rivers and lakes. The water turns into gas, or vapour, and rises up into the atmosphere. Eventually, some of it cools and forms clouds of water droplets. The droplets gradually get bigger until they are too heavy to stay as clouds. Then they fall back on to the earth as snow, hail or rain.

Some of the water soaks deep into the ground to feed wells underground and streams. Other water runs off the land into lakes or rivers. Some will even be collected in containers and used as drinking water.

Water around the world

Although there is enough fresh water overall on the earth for everyone's needs, rain does not fall evenly over all the world. Some places do not have enough water, while others have more than people need. Because water is 'on tap' in many homes, offices and factories, some people do not think it is precious, and use too much.

Some people in the world have only dirty water for washing and drinking. It may contain organisms that can make them ill.

World water facts

- One-fifth of the world's people do not have safe drinking water.
- In Europe and America, 95% of the population has fresh clean drinking water 'on tap'.
- In Africa and Asia, fewer than 10% of people have clean drinking water from wells and tanks.

River features

Most rivers start as small streams, often high up in hills or mountains. Here the water usually flows quite fast. As rivers develop they get wider and slower. They often carry fine mud, called silt, that has been washed from the river banks.

When rivers, such as the Nile in Egypt, flood they leave silt on flood plains. This makes the soil fertile.

Near the sea, rivers become wide and wind through a flat area called a flood plain. When some rivers reach the coast they form a delta. This is a fan-shaped area where the river splits into many channels before reaching the sea.

River facts

World's longest river:
River Nile (Bar el-Nid), Sudan–Egypt = 6670 km
World's shortest river:
D River, Lincoln City, Oregon = 37 m (+ or - 5 m)
Longest ship canal:
Suez Canal, Egypt = 161.9 km

The importance of rivers

Rivers can be beautiful places, and provide a habitat for many plants and animals. They are also useful to people: for water in the home, farming, transport, industry and recreation.

River water is a shared resource. What is done to a river in one place may affect it a long way downstream, so we need to be careful about how we use rivers – for our own needs, for others, and for the wildlife that depends on them.

River life

The Pokot people live in north-west Kenya. They are semi nomadic people, moving around to find food for their herds of goats and cattle.

For some of the time, they live near the Moruny River at a place called Marich Pass. Although they share the river with crocodiles, and the river banks with leopard and other creatures, they build small round huts called *bandas* near the river. Living near the river, they can use the running water for all their needs.

The river provides water for washing, drinking and for cooking. One of their foods is a type of soaked grain. It is put in a wooden cradle and placed in the river water until it is soft and ready to eat. The Pokot also catch fish and birds for food.

At Marich the river is broad and shallow for most of the year. Sand banks separate channels of water making safe places to water the livestock.

The Pokot people have not changed or spoiled the river environment. This is partly because there are not many of them, but mainly it is because the people are careful with the river as they depend on it so much.

The Moruny River is in Kenya. Where it is very shallow, the Pokot people use it as a route-way to walk to other villages.

7

River Flora and Fauna

Wherever rivers are found in the world they provide a home for plants, insects, birds and animals. Each river habitat is a finely balanced system that supports a series of food webs.

Food webs

In the natural world, every animal eats a variety of food. Some animals eat plants, and some eat other animals. The patterns of who eats what are known as food webs.

For example, some plants are eaten by fish, and fish may be eaten by birds. The birds may then be eaten by a fox, or people.

Flora

Plants that grow in and near rivers come in all shapes and sizes. Tiny organisms that live near the surface, such as algae, are very important food for small animals and fish. Larger plants, such as rushes, provide habitats and nesting places for animals and birds. Some trees, such as willows, like a lot of water, so they are often found on river banks.

Not many plants grow in the faster flowing parts of a river. This is because there is not much food in the water for plants to feed on. Where the river is wider and slower, there is more food and so more plant life.

Water lilies on the River Amazon in Brazil. The leaves are nearly 1 metre across.

Fauna

A healthy river habitat provides food, shelter and nest sites for insects, fish, birds and animals. Some river fauna, such as fish, live in the river water. Others live on the banks but feed in the river. Still others visit the river just for drinking water.

Creatures and birds that live in and around rivers may have specially adapted features for their habitat. For example, some have 'waterproofing' in their fur or feathers. Others have webbed feet for paddling or long beaks for digging in mud.

Otters have strong, short legs and webbed paws for swimming.

Some birds such as kingfishers live on fish they catch in rivers.

Healthy river

A clean healthy stream or river should contain some of the plants, animals and insects below. Use a reference book to see what they look like.

PLANTS	ANIMALS
Bulrushes	Stonefly nymph
Flowering rushes	Freshwater shrimp
Water milfoil	Leech
Perfoliate pondweed	Crayfish
	Swimming mayfly nymph
INSECTS	Cased caddis larva
Alder fly	Flat worm
Damsel flies	River limpet
	Peacockle

Rivers near the coast

Most rivers are largely filled by fresh water. However, as a river nears the sea, salt water is washed by the tides into the mouth of the river. This is called an estuary. Where the fresh and salt water mix is known as 'brackish' water.

Rubbish dropped in rivers can kill wildlife. However, sometimes animals adapt to these new surroundings. The following things were found in the River Hudson, New York, by fishermen:

- **Tyres caked in mud and filled with worms, mud crabs, barnacles, sea squirts and anemones.**
- **A wine glass covered in barnacles.**
- **A shoe, with a crayfish living in it.**

The brackish zone sees the most changes in its daily cycle. There are constant changes in the depth of the water and in the speed of water flow.

Animals tend to avoid this brackish zone, preferring either the freshwater or the sea environments. Even so, all around the world, estuaries support a huge variety of life.

For example, in the estuary of the River Thames, in Britain, it is possible to find about thirty different types of invertebrate creatures, including shore crabs, water snails and shrimps.

Many wading birds live on estuaries where they dig for food in the rich mud.

The Sundarbans

The River Ganges flows through India and Bangladesh and forms a delta on the Bay of Bengal. This area includes more than fifty islands and is called the Sundarbans.

The Sundarbans contains the largest area of mangrove trees in the world. A mangrove swamp is like a forest on stilts. The mangrove tree roots run through the air and water down into the ground below. Eighty per cent of the land is under water at high tide. The mangroves keep the soil of the delta from being washed away.

The Sundarbans gets its name from sundari trees that once grew there in great numbers. They grew to 25 metres tall, and were used for building or making boats. Now, they have almost all been cut down.

However, the area was made into a wildlife sanctuary in 1966. It is home to many rare, endangered and protected animals and birds, including Bengal tigers, crocodiles, spotted deer and golden eagles.

Mangrove forests are found on estuaries in warm climates. They are home to many fish and animals, including crocodiles.

Rivers in Flood

Some rivers flood regularly. Floods occur when snow melts, or there has been a large amount of rain. Extra water flows down the river and spreads out over the flat flood plain and delta areas. This can ruin crops and sometimes whole towns and villages are washed away.

However, when flood water goes down, it leaves behind rich silt that was carried by the river. This makes the soil very fertile so that it is good for farming.

A flood in Hanoi, Vietnam. The city is located on the delta of the Red River.

For thousands of years, people have tried to control flooding. On flood plains, people build banks along the sides of rivers to keep the water in. Specially built ditches and canals may help drain excess water away.

However, sometimes these alterations can actually make flooding worse. When there are banks along the river, it sometimes starts to fill up with silt. This makes the level of the river bed rise, so that the banks are not high enough to keep in all the water. The danger of flooding becomes greater than before the banks were built.

Rivers near coasts can also flood when there is a very high sea tide. Because land around river estuaries is often flat, it is easy for it to be covered by flood water.

The Thames Barrier

London, a city of more than 7 million people, has a large flood barrier, built across the River Thames. Its job is to protect London from being flooded if a very big tide comes in from the North Sea. If the barrier was not there, thousands of homes and businesses could find themselves under water.

Each section of the barrier can be controlled from either bank of the river. Every part of the machinery has two separate controls so that it is almost impossible for it to fail.

Jan Colby has worked on the Thames Barrier for 14 years. His job is to make sure that every piece of machinery is regularly checked and tested. When he is not at work he is always on call for emergencies, even on Christmas day.

Jan says: 'If there is an emergency – that is, a flood tide – then the closure team meets in the control room. We have to check that other barriers and gates are also closed to make sure that everyone in London will be safe. Within an hour all the gates are shut.'

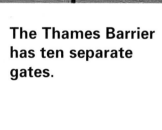

The Thames Barrier has ten separate gates.

Jan Colby is in charge of making sure the Thames Barrier works properly.

Working Rivers

As rivers flow, they have no natural barriers. Some, like the River Rhine and the River Danube in Europe, flow through many countries on their way from their source to the sea. Every activity or use of the river has an effect on both people and wildlife, which often continues a long way downstream.

Transport

Rivers provide ready-made transport routes. Many of the world's rivers provide a route to move goods and people, using anything from small boats to huge ocean-going ships. Some rivers are the easiest way, or even the only way, to travel through an area. For example, the Amazon River in Brazil is surrounded by dense rain forest and there are few roads. The river is used as a main 'road'.

This family in the Amazon rain forest live by a river. The only way they can travel around is by boat.

Ports, where boats load and unload, grew up on rivers. Ports are not always located on coasts. Many are situated inland, as far as ships or boats can go. They were often the beginning of a new settlement or industry.

Altering rivers

Some rivers and streams have had their courses altered to make it easier for people to travel on them. Canals were built to link up major rivers, to make transportation of goods and materials quicker between industrial areas.

Some canals were made by just straightening the river. Others were built specially to provide a transport route, and then filled with river water.

Activity

Loading safety levels for ships

Many tonnes of cargo are carried by boat on rivers and canals. Boats have to be carefully loaded so that they do not sink, or become dangerous. Here is an experiment to try. You will need:

- A boat. Some plastic food boxes make a good flat-bottomed barge, or you can make your own boat.
- Some stones, marbles or blocks, for cargo.
- A waterproof marker pen.
- A sink or water tank.

1 Float your boat in a tank of fresh water.
2 Load it until you think it has a safe load, and will not carry any more cargo.
3 Mark the water level on the outside of your barge with the marker pen.
4 Count the number of marbles or blocks.

Repeat this experiment in a tank of very salty water. Do you think the water will make a difference? From this experiment, how do you think boats should be loaded at sea compared with boats on the fresh water of rivers or lakes?

▶ An old mill wheel at a ruined mill on the upper part of the River Seine, in France.

▼ Trees used to grow where this reservoir was built in Australia. These trees cannot live in water, so now they are dead.

Rivers and power

River water was used to power machines from Roman times until the invention of steam engines in the eighteenth century. Water from a river turned a mill wheel. The wheel drove machines which could, for example, grind grain or saw timber.

Now the power of flowing water is harnessed to generate electricity, called hydroelectric power. To make power, water must be flowing from a higher place to a lower place. A dam is built across a river, and the water collects behind it in a reservoir. The water flows down through turbines that make electricity, and into the river below the dam.

Although water power is reasonably clean, river environments are affected. Building a dam and filling a reservoir changes the landscape. Plants and animals may die, and people may have to move away. Downstream, there may be less water in the river, which changes wildlife habitats and makes farmland less fertile.

Water for people

Much of the world's drinking water is taken from rivers. The water must be cleaned before it can be used safely for drinking or washing.

In many places, dirty water and waste is poured straight into rivers, or the sea. This pollutes the water with organisms that can cause serious diseases, such as typhoid fever, cholera and dysentery. Water from industry may contain poisonous chemicals, metals and oils. Why is there so much waste in the first place? Perhaps people need to think about ways of reducing the amount of waste they produce.

Rubbish and sewage has polluted this river in Spain.

The amount of fresh water in the world is limited. However, demand for water keeps growing. If people continue to pollute it, or use too much, soon there may not be enough for everyone. We will have to find ways of using less, or using water in different ways.

The effects of industry

Many factories are located along rivers. Some let their waste flow directly into the river. Other industries may dump waste that contains chemicals and metals directly on to the land. Rain washes them into the soil, and eventually the ground water finds its way into springs and rivers.

Industrial waste often contains poisonous chemicals such as arsenic, lead and mercury. When chemicals get into rivers, they later find their way into drinking water. Scientists are worried that drinking even small amounts of these chemicals over many years may have harmful effects on people and animals.

Another type of pollution is caused by industries that use large amounts of water to cool machinery. Heat from the machines makes the water hot. When it is put back into a river or lake, the heated water can kill some kinds of plants and fish.

A petrol terminal on the River Rhine in Switzerland.

River disaster

On 25th April, 1998, a disaster struck southern Spain, near the city of Seville. A reservoir at a mine broke its banks, sending a huge amount of poisonous sludge into the nearby Guadiamar River. Thousands of fish and birds were killed. It was thought that 20 million tonnes of mud would have to be cleared up.

Unfortunately, the mine is near the Doñana National Park, Europe's largest nature reserve. About 6 million birds migrate there each year, and it is home to lynx, otters, eagles and other wildlife. A system of emergency earth walls were built to keep the flow of mud out of the park, and send it into the larger Guadalquivir River. Even so, environmentalists believed that the chemicals would get into the park.

Many farmers saw their crops ruined. Large fields of tomatoes, fruit, olives and cotton were stained black. The land will be infertile for 25 years because of the spill. People living along the rivers were warned not to drink water from wells, as the poisons would have seeped into the ground water.

It will be many years before the rivers and surrounding area will recover. Environmentalists think there could be problems for up to 40 years.

When poisonous sludge polluted the Guadiamar River in Spain, the dead fish were collected up immediately. This was to stop them being eaten by other animals, and to prevent poisons getting into the natural food webs.

Farming

Farming is often located around rivers, because their valleys and plains provide fertile land for growing crops. In dry regions, farmers use river water to irrigate their land. They dig irrigation ditches to bring water from a river to the farmland, or they use pumps and pipes to extract it from the river. This can reduce the flow of water downstream causing important wetlands and marshes to dry up, leaving water birds fewer places to feed and nest.

Farmers use chemicals. Fertilizers make the soil more fertile, pesticides are poisons that kill harmful insects, and herbicides get rid of weeds. Water from rain or snow can wash all these chemicals into rivers.

Animal waste also causes problems. Factory farming of cattle, pigs and chickens produces large quantities of manure. When the manure, and fertilizers, find their way into rivers they encourage bacteria and algae to grow. Where fertilizers get washed into the river, reed beds soak them up and may die. This removes many nesting sites that are used by water birds.

So much algae has grown on this stream that it is impossible to see the water.

Oxygen in rivers

Nearly all living things need oxygen to live. Oxygen is found in water. When sewage or fertilizers get into the water they become food for tiny organisms, such as bacteria or algae. These multiply very quickly, and use the oxygen in the river. This does not leave enough for other living things, such as fish. The fish, and other animals, either move away, or they die from lack of oxygen.

Activity

Checking pollution

By taking water samples from a stream or river, it is easy to find out the level of pollution. Many of the small creatures that live in the water are good 'indicators' of pollution.

Carefully collect a sample of water from your test area. Remember you are collecting live creatures, so keep them safely and return them to the river as soon as you can.

Use the chart below to help you find out if your stream or river is healthy. All the creatures below live in clean water, but only the bloodworm and rat-tailed maggot also live in dirty water.
- Badly polluted water: Rat-tailed maggot only.
- Polluted water: Bloodworm and rat-tailed maggot.
- Clean, slow flowing water: Freshwater shrimp.
- Clean, fast flowing water: Stonefly nymphs.

If you discover by your test that your water is polluted, what could be the cause? If you discover by your test that the water is clean, how can you make sure that it stays unpolluted ?

List three ways that you can help to keep streams and rivers clean and healthy.

A simple water-wise safety code
Always:
- Make sure someone responsible knows where you are going.
- Work in pairs or a group.
- Wear sensible clothing and shoes.
- Follow the country code.
- Stay out of the water.
- Avoid steep and slippery banks.
- Leave the area undisturbed.

LIVE IN CLEAN AND POLLUTED WATER   **DO NOT LIVE IN POLLUTED WATER**

Rat-tailed maggot   **Bloodworm**   **Freshwater shrimp**   **Stonefly nymph**

Recreation and Tourism

Most people live in towns and cities and many enjoy visits to rivers and water parks. A river bank can be a quiet, restful place where wildlife can be seen. Birdwatching and fishing are popular pastimes.

People who fish enjoy the peace and quiet of the river bank.

Fishing can hurt wildlife if people are not careful. For example, fishing lines thrown away on a river bank can get tangled around birds' wings, legs and beaks, harming or even killing them. Animals and birds can be poisoned if they swallow lead fishing weights.

Wetlands in danger

People also like to use rivers and their surroundings for energetic activities such as sailing, boating, walking or cycling. This often means that river banks are damaged, water is polluted and much of the wildlife goes into hiding.

Even activities that seem quite simple and harmless can change a river for ever. River banks may be worn away by people walking or cycling, or they may be damaged by the 'wash' from motor boats travelling too fast. Sometimes, people leave litter or pick rare plants and flowers.

Development on rivers

Once a river becomes popular with visitors it may become a 'tourist area'. This is when major changes take place. For example, special paths may be made for walkers, cyclists, and people in wheelchairs. Car parks are built; cafés, shops, boatyards and fuel stations open. Sometimes, hotels are built for tourists.

People can enjoy themselves, but it may be more difficult for rare animals and plants to survive. The only way to keep a natural environment is to set aside land for national parks and conservation areas. In these areas, development is more strictly controlled.

Beautiful river areas often attract many people.

The Everglades

Some river areas are managed in national parks. For example, the Everglades in Florida, USA, has been a national park for over 50 years.

The Everglades contains marshes, islands, mangroves, and wet grasslands. A river flows through the park which is like no other. It is 97 km wide, 485 km long, and seldom more than 60 cm deep. There are no currents in the river, and the human eye cannot see any movement of the water.

A huge variety of wildlife lives there, including fish, deer, pelicans, snakes, alligators and cougars.

Air boats can travel easily across the water plants in the Everglades, but they cause damage.

Many tourists visit the Everglades. They are taken on sight-seeing tours using air boats. However, the boats are noisy and fast. They can damage not only the soil and plants, but often hurt a rare animal, the manatee, which is slow moving and cannot escape in time.

Can planning help?

Local, national and global planning authorities are now looking very closely at all development and building that people are planning near rivers. They often carry out environmental studies to see what damage would take place, or how wildlife would be affected.

Activity

What happens to the river bank?

Imagine you live near the river in this photo. Or, think of a natural area of river near your home or school. Pretend that the land next to the river is up for sale. Everyone who lives nearby has different ideas about what should happen to it. What issues need to be discussed?

Try a role-play activity:

- You are the local planner.
- You are a farmer whose land is on the opposite bank.
- You are a family of animals that live on the riverbank.
- You are a businessman who wants to build a water-sports centre.
- You are a local builder who needs work.
- You live nearby and want the land to be turned into a park.

This beautiful river is in the Catskill Mountains in the USA.

Staying in your role, talk about how the changes might affect you. Can you decide what is best to do with the land?

After the role play, talk about all the different points of view. Were some people more persuasive than others? Was it possible to agree on what to do?

Taking Care of Rivers

As we saw at the beginning of this book, water is a precious resource that needs to be conserved. Keeping rivers clean and healthy is an important part of looking after the Earth's water supplies.

However, it is not just water that is at stake. If people do not take active care of rivers, farming will be threatened, and relaxing on rivers may not be pleasant, or even possible. And most importantly, there will not be the variety of plants and wildlife that exists today.

Taking action

All around the world there are environment agencies that work to protect river environments. However, it is not just the job of rangers to care for clean water and healthy rivers. You can help in your local area. Look out for evidence to see whether rivers and streams are being protected, or not:

- Are river banks free from rubbish?
- Is there damage to plants and animal life?
- Are there signs of pollution?

If you think there is a problem with your local river, contact the river authority.

The Clearwater Project

The 'Clearwater Project' takes people sailing on the Hudson River in New York state, USA, aboard the *Clearwater*, a 32-metre wooden sailing boat.

They use a fishing net to bring up a wide variety of species that live in the river. By examining and even touching the creatures and plant life, just out of their natural habitat, visitors can see how they survive (or try to survive) in their environment.

After they spend just a few hours out on the Hudson River, people begin to feel a sense of responsibility for its well-being and conservation. They realise that everyone can take an active role, helping to conserve and preserve our natural resources.

Allyson Bizer, an education specialist who works on the project, says: 'Thousands of people come on the boat each year. It is my job to teach them about the Hudson. The biggest challenge is to give people hope. The visitors on the *Clearwater* need to learn about how rivers become polluted and that we cannot eat the fish, but also they need to find out and explore ways that they too can help combat or control problems in the future.

'However, they also need to have fun and enjoy the "great outdoors". On the *Clearwater* we certainly do!'

Allyson Bizer on board the *Clearwater*. She is holding a fish called a sturgeon, caught in the River Hudson.

Keeping a balance

People will always want to change the world around them. They will always need new houses, buildings and industry. However many of these changes will affect water supply and the 'health' of a river. It is important to find a balance between preserving the natural environment and allowing some changes to take place.

If we take care of rivers, they will continue to be the beautiful places we can enjoy today.

Upstream – Downstream

The game on the right shows some of the ways that a river can be affected by people. It is for two to four people to play. You can play the game in either direction: from source to sea, or from the coast to the source.

You will need the game, a dice marked one to six and a counter for each player. You must throw an exact number to finish.

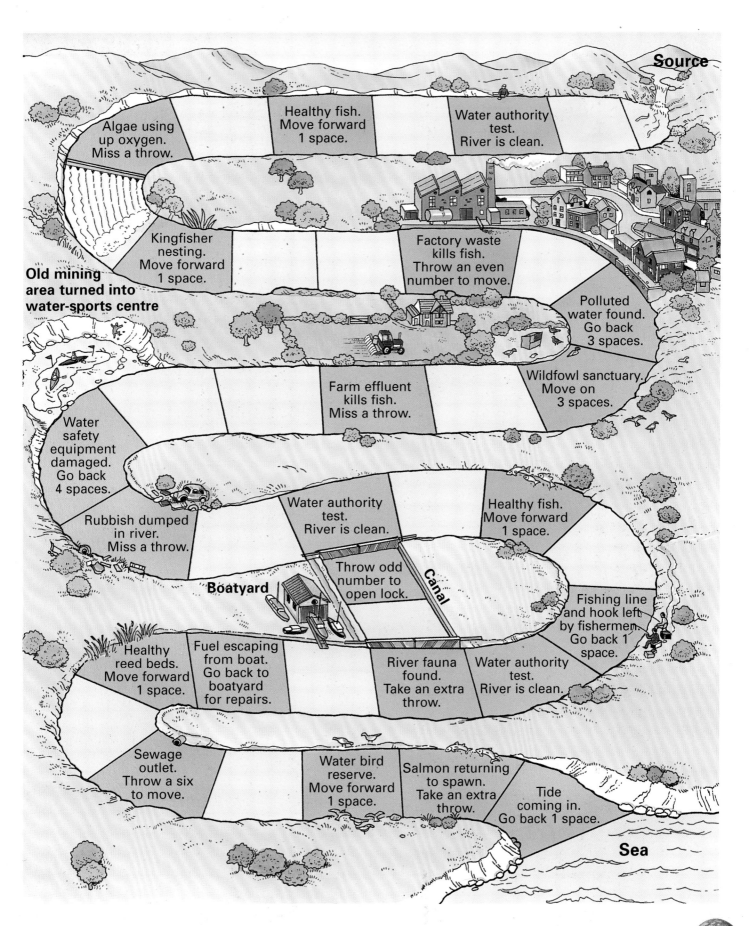

Source

Water authority test. River is clean.

Healthy fish. Move forward 1 space.

Algae using up oxygen. Miss a throw.

Kingfisher nesting. Move forward 1 space.

Factory waste kills fish. Throw an even number to move.

Polluted water found. Go back 3 spaces.

Old mining area turned into water-sports centre

Farm effluent kills fish. Miss a throw.

Wildfowl sanctuary. Move on 3 spaces.

Water safety equipment damaged. Go back 4 spaces.

Rubbish dumped in river. Miss a throw.

Water authority test. River is clean.

Healthy fish. Move forward 1 space.

Boatyard

Throw odd number to open lock.

Canal

Fishing line and hook left by fishermen. Go back 1 space.

Healthy reed beds. Move forward 1 space.

Fuel escaping from boat. Go back to boatyard for repairs.

River fauna found. Take an extra throw.

Water authority test. River is clean.

Sewage outlet. Throw a six to move.

Water bird reserve. Move forward 1 space.

Salmon returning to spawn. Take an extra throw.

Tide coming in. Go back 1 space.

Sea

29

Glossary

Algae   Simple plants. Most of them live in water.

Bacteria   Tiny organisms, some of which are harmful and cause diseases.

Cargo   Goods carried by ship, or by aircraft.

Conservation   Taking care of the environment to make sure that people, animals and plants always have everything they need to live.

Conserve   To keep from harm.

Dam   A wall built to hold back water.

Development   Gradual growth and change.

Downstream   In the direction that a river or stream flows.

Environment   Everything in our surroundings: the earth, air and water.

Estuary   The mouth of a river at the sea where fresh water meets sea water.

Factory farming   Rearing many animals together in buildings. Pigs or chickens are often raised in this way.

Fauna   Animals in a particular region.

Fertilizer   Something added to soil to make it more fertile or productive.

Flood   When a lot of water covers land that is normally dry.

Flora   Plants in a particular region.

Habitat   The natural home of a plant or animal.

Industry   Making or manufacturing things, usually in factories.

Infertile   Not able to grow anything.

Invertebrate   A small animal that does not have a backbone.

Manure   Waste from animals.

Organisms   Living animals or plants.

Pesticide   A chemical that kills pests, usually insects.

Plain   A flat, level area of land.

Pollution   Damage to air, water or land by harmful materials.

Recreation   Doing something for relaxation or for pleasure.

Sewage   The liquid waste that is carried away from homes and factories.

Source   The place where a stream or river starts.

Tides   The rise and fall of the sea on the shore.

Upstream   In the direction opposite to the way a river or stream flows.

Topic Web and Resources

MUSIC
- 'The Moldau' by Smetana
- Handel's 'Water Music'

GEOGRAPHY
- Physical features of rivers
- River profile
- Tourism and recreation
- Environmental issues: eg, erosion, pollution
- Conservation
- Atlas skills: plot the course of a major river.

HISTORY
- Exploration linked to rivers
- Water transport
- Industrial Revolution and water power

ART & CRAFT
- Using rivers as a stimulus for drawing/painting
- Design a poster for river conservation

Topic Web
RIVERS

DESIGN AND TECHNOLOGY
- Water wheels and mills
- Design of boats
- Dams and locks

MATHS
- Data collection
- Measurement of capacity
- Tally chart of river boats, barges, etc.

SCIENCE
- States of water: solid, liquid and gas
- Forces: gravity
- Water cycle
- Floating and sinking
- Biology: flora and fauna, food chains
- Environmental issues: eg water contamination

ENGLISH
- Story: *Wind in the Willows*
- Creative writing
- Appropriate poetry
- Library skills

Other resources

Books
Design and Make: Water Projects by John Williams, (Wayland, 1997).
Natural Cycles: The Water Cycle by David Smith (Wayland, 1994).
Protecting Our Planet: Keeping Water Clean by Ewan McLeish (Wayland, 1997).
Take 5: Rivers by Steve Parker (Franklin Watts, 1997).
The World's Rivers series (Wayland, 1992–93).
Great Rivers series by Michael Pollard (Evans Brothers, 1997).

Multimedia
Exploring Water Habitats, Wayland 1997.

Internet sites
The Clearwater Project home page can be found at http://www.clearwater.org

Places to visit

The Royal Society for the Protection of Birds owns and manages many nature reserves situated on rivers. For information, telephone 01767 680551 or see its website at www.rspb.org.uk.

Cuckmere River Valley, Seven Sisters Country Park, near Eastbourne: river estuary and natural meanders, education centre.
Galloway Hydro Visitors Centre, Tongland Power Station, Kirkcudbright, Galloway: tours of hydroelectric power station and dam.
Ironbridge Museum of the Water, Telford.
National Waterways Museum, Gloucester.
River Tees Valley, Stockton-on-Tees. Tours arranged to High Force waterfall and new Tees barrage.
Thames Barrier Visitor Centre, Woolwich, London: contains interactive displays on the River Thames, its history, ecology and development, and also a working model of the Thames Barrier.

Index